Go Greek

The Sorority Recruitment Survival Guide

Greek Life Now

www.greeklifenow.com

~ 3 ~

Thank You

I would like to dedicate this book to all of my Greek sisters. In particular thank you to the girls that were there to help me through recruitment and eventually became my closest sisters. There is a bond between us that could never be broken. A big shout out to my Greek family. We now span many generations, multiple campuses, and you continue to be my biggest supporters. Lastly, I would like to thank the chapter that I call home. All of the alumna and active sisters have truly shown me how one can support a dream and make it reality.

DLAM

Table of Contents

So You Want to Go Greek...

Do you want the chance to create special memories that you will never forget? Do you love to give back to the community and want to create opportunities for yourself? Do you want to form solid friendships that will last a lifetime? It looks like sorority life is for you!

Many girls go away to college and don't know many people in their new city. Being on your own can be scary, especially if you don't have a good support system, so you might want to join a sorority to make new friends. You might have been really involved in high school. Maybe you're worried about finding ways to get involved as a leader on campus. You might want to join a sorority to be part of a significant organization and to find opportunities for involvement throughout campus. Maybe you were service driven in high school. You might want to join a sorority to find a way to give back to your community and to affect people across the nation by

contributing to incredible charitable organizations.

There are so many different reasons to join a

sorority in college, and the girls who go through the

process of recruitment are all different. These girls come

from different cities, states, backgrounds, and families, but

they all come together to participate in a tradition of

sisterhood and become part of many different incredible

organizations.

A sorority is a society that is composed of women who

share common interests and traits. There are 123

fraternities and sororities in the world, with 9 million

members in total. There are a lot of things you might not

have known about Greek life and its members:

- All of the Apollo 11 astronauts were Greek
  members

- 7 out of 10 people listed in Who's Who are Greek members

- Of North America's 50 largest corporations, 43 are headed by men and women who are Greek members, 30% of all Fortune 500's

There are many common misconceptions surrounding the idea of sorority life. Movies and TV shows imply that sororities are full of ditzy, rich and snobby girls who are only interested in parties, boys and generally having a good time. However, this is not true. Sorority members (commonly known as sisters) are hardworking, supportive, and charitable individuals. There are various benefits that come with being part of a sorority:

- Creating strong friendships between other members who will grow to become your sisters and closest friends. They will support you and be behind you, no matter what.

- Furthering your leadership abilities. In your sorority, you'll learn how to motivate others, public speaking, budget managing and how to run effective meetings. These are essential skills that can help you throughout life - inside and outside of your university.

- Develop high scholastic achievement. Your sorority will guide you through your college years, offering strong support and tutoring. Academic achievement is a very important factor of sorority life, with members of sororities achieving a much greater graduation rate, around 20% higher than average.

- Opportunities to relax and socialize. Throughout the year, you will participate in many social events,

such as Homecoming, Greek Week and Parent's
Weekend. These will bring you closer to your
sisters and open opportunities to meet new
people, especially from other sororities and
fraternities.

- Helping the community. Each sorority organizes
philanthropies, which are projects organized to
benefit the surrounding community. Sorority
members have strong enthusiasm and
commitment for community service and it's an
important part of sorority life. Over $7 million is
raised each year by sororities and fraternities with
10 million hours of volunteer hours in total each
year.

- Personal health and fitness. Each sorority and
fraternity participates in numerous competitive
sports. They also take part in numerous Greek

tournaments against other sororities and fraternities. These activities are designed to keep you active and on your feet – an essential part of a healthy lifestyle.

- A bright future. In today's economy, it is hard to find that dream career that you have been looking for. You'll need more than just qualifications. Using resources from alumni, you may find the career you were looking for. Furthermore, the skills you've enhanced through your time in the sorority will provide you with key abilities that employers are looking for.

You may be a little unsure about this whole recruitment thing, but even if you are just considering recruitment and wondering if it's right for you, you should give this process a shot. As you go into different houses and meet the girls who belong to them you will get a clearer picture of whether or not sorority life is really for you. Just give

recruitment a chance, and I'm sure you will see what

amazing opportunities and experiences lay in store for you

within Greek life!

It's Just Greek to Me

Bump: the transition that occurs when a PNM is talking to a chapter woman and is interrupted by another chapter woman who then begins a new conversation with the PNM. This rush tactic is employed to allow multiple sisters to get to know a PNM and form an opinion of them.

Continuous Open Bidding – the process in which a PNM can be offered a bid after the formal recruitment process has ended.

Date Functions – a social event in which chapter women bring their own date (rather than a mixer/fraternity social in which only men from that fraternity are invited). These functions often are themed and may occur off-campus. This is similar to formal, but typically more casual.

Dirty Rushing – occurs when a sorority house or one sorority sister breaks a rule by doing something to have unfair influence over rushees. For example promising a girl a bid, telling her she will be her little sister, giving a rushee a gift, etc.

<u>Dropped</u>- term referring to a house's decision to not invite a PNM back to visit for the next round. Also refers to the PNM's decision to turn down an invitation to visit a house. When a girl drops out of sorority recruitment that means she has completely withdrawn from the recruitment process and is ineligible for a bid.

<u>Dues</u>- fees paid to the organization you are affiliated with. Dues must be paid to remain in "good standing" with your chapter.

<u>E-Board</u>- *Executive Board*, also referred to in some sororities as Executive Council, which includes the elected executive officers of the chapter (i.e. President, Vice Presidents, Secretary, etc.).

<u>Fraternity Sweetheart/ Dream Girl</u>- a chapter woman who is elected by the members of a fraternity to represent its members, often by appearing on their chapter's composite for that year. The Sweetheart/Dream Girl is usually chosen for her dedication and contributions to the success

of the chapter over the previous year, and is encouraged to wear the fraternity's letters.

GDI – *God Damn Independent*; term referring to college students who are not in a fraternity or sorority. This term is used proudly by the non-Greeks themselves in some colleges, but is often considered a negative or insulting term.

Greek Week- a week in which all of the Greek organizations on campus come together for activities and friendly competitions.

Hot Boxing – usually not permitted during formal recruitment; a situation in which multiple chapter women are talking to a PNM at one time. This can be intimidating, making the PNM feel uncomfortable and overwhelmed.

House Mom- officially titled House Director; refers to a person hired to manage the sorority house and supervise the home operations.

<u>Lavaliere</u>- necklace bearing the letters of a fraternity/sorority.

<u>Legacy</u> – A PNM who is closely related to a woman with membership in a National Panhellenic member sorority. The definition of a legacy varies from sorority to sorority, but it almost always includes a woman whose mother, sister, aunt or grandmother was a member of a particular sorority. Legacies are usually given special consideration for membership, but sororities are not required to invite them to membership.

<u>Panhellenic Council</u>- the governing body that oversees the cooperation of the member sororities. This is the local body of the larger National Panhellenic Council. Also known as Panhel, this council is made up of officers elected from the various sororities on campus.

<u>Philanthropy</u> – an active effort, project or service to promote human welfare or the raising of funds to be donated for that purpose.

Potential New Member (PNM) – also known as Rushees, these are the women going through Membership Recruitment in hopes of joining a sorority.

Preference (Prefs) – the final round of formal recruitment events which is more intimate and formal than previous rounds. Immediately after the preference events, the PNMs complete their final ranking of sororities in preferential order.

Recommendation – letters sent to chapters by either active or alumni Greeks on behalf of a PNM that they are acquainted with. Usually note why a PNM may be a great or not so great fit for a particular chapter.

Recruitment Counselor – formerly known as Rush Counselors and sometimes referred to as Pi Chis or Rho Gammas; sorority women who disaffiliate from their own chapter during Recruitment to help the Potential New Members with the selection process in an unbiased fashion. They offer impartial support and answer questions during Membership Recruitment as they lead PNMs from party to party.

Ritual – the sacred ceremonies practiced by every chapter of a Greek letter organization, generally secret.

Rounds – events organized during recruitment with varying degrees of formality and exclusion in which PNMs have the opportunity to meet with each chapter.

Rush Crush- when a sister and a rushee really connect it is said that the sorority sister has a "rush crush" on the rushee. Girls may have a "rush crush" on one house or a sister in the house. Sometimes rush crushes become big and little sisters, but sadly sometimes a rush crush is one sided and the girl goes to a different sorority.

Snap Bid – associated with continuous open bidding; a time in which chapters contact ladies who did not attend, single preferred, or otherwise dropped out to see if they would like to join a chapter with room permitting.

<u>Stitched Letter</u>- Greek letters that are actually sewn on a shirt or bag. Some chapters have rules regarding the point in their membership period that New Members are allowed to wear stitched letters. For example, in some chapters you have to be an initiated member to wear the stitched letters.

<u>Suicide Bid</u> – a PNM who intentionally indicates that she wishes to only attend one chapter's preference. This is highly discouraged and is not allowed at some schools.

Spring or Fall: That is the Question

Sororities governed by the National Panhellenic Conference usually hold a recruitment period for potential new members, at most, twice a year – once in the fall and again in the spring. There are two types of recruitment periods (commonly known as rushes), formal recruitment and COB (Continuous Open Bidding). Some colleges kick off the rush seasons with an opening fair complete with activities and food. Each sorority participating in the rush season will have a booth, where you can learn more about the chapter.

Formal recruitment is the main recruitment season of the year for PNMs (potential new members) and commonly occurs in the fall semester; however this may vary between different sororities and universities. It usually consists of 3-5 events early in the semester or just prior to the start of the semester. These rounds include; philanthropy rounds, where you'll learn more about which charitable organizations the sororities support, video rounds where you'll learn more about the sisterhood, what they stand for and their activities within society and lastly, preference rounds where each sorority obtains the chance to reveal how much the sorority means to them.

During the formal recruitment process, groups of rushees are led by girls affiliated with each sorority, called pi chis or rho gammas. These girls are a great first-hand source to find out more information about going Greek. These pi chis or rho gammas are there for the PNMs throughout the whole recruitment process. At the end of the formal recruitment period, sororities give out 'bids' to PNMs as invites to their sorority. Formal recruitment is a big event in the calendar, with new members rushing into their sister's arms and big after parties being held usually.

The majority of students tend to rush in the fall, during the formal recruitment period. This is due to many factors:

- All sorority houses are open to new members during the formal recruitment process
- New member education may consist of various tasks that may be found easier to each individual when completed as a larger class.
- They feel that it will give them an opportunity to meet new people and establish good friendships.

Although it may seem that fall is a very beneficial time to be a rushee, there are many disadvantages. Many potential new members comment on the overcrowding of fall rush. This is to be expected, with many freshmen entering the universities and starting their first semesters.

Also, many don't feel satisfied with their knowledge of how each sorority is represented in the college and local communities and how they work. This is a drawback that halts many potential new members from participating in the formal recruitment period in fall, and influences them to participate in a rush in spring. Furthermore, there are numerous reasons as to why people would not rush in fall, such as; they want to independently meet a wide variety of new people without the help of a rush and that they may not find the time to rush in the fall due to other college events, studying or they may not feel confident enough to rush straight away.

Continuous open bidding, more commonly known as COB, can occur at any given time in the school calendar, most commonly in spring. Sororities can only open themselves to continuous open bidding if they have some spare places left over from the formal recruitment period. There are many advantages to continuous open bidding, such as;

- It is informal, therefore there aren't as many rules or pressure on what to wear or how to act. It is a more relaxed atmosphere that helps you feel more comfortable.

- After you've been on campus for the fall, you'll have an idea of the reputations of all the sororities and the type of people in them. This will provide you with a further insight into which sorority you wish to join.

- After being on campus for a while without being part of a sorority, you would have gained some friends. Gaining friends before joining a sorority might increase you social circle more.

- There is less competition for places as less people compete for them.

Even though there are many benefits to participating in a rush that is a continuous open bidding, there are also some disadvantages. The main disadvantage was mentioned earlier, that it is extremely rare that all the sororities on campus are participating in an extra informal rush after the formal recruitment. Therefore you may have to wait until formal recruitment next fall to attempt to join a certain sorority that may be on your mind. Also, you may not obtain the benefits that come with formal recruitment. Within formal recruitment, you are guided through the process by pi chis or rho gammas. These are rarely available throughout spring rush; therefore you will have less guidance during the process. Also, spring rush is not as big of a deal as formal recruitment. Hence, the transition into the sorority may not start with extravagant parties as it would do with formal recruitment.

Additionally, you may not receive the overall view of sorority life in the sororities that are accepting new members due to the lesser time limit spent in each sorority house, compared to the formal recruitment period. These may lead to an uninformed decision on what sorority you truly want to join.

Each semesters' recruitments have strengths and weaknesses, and one is not better than the other. There are two very different types of recruitment, and each appeal to very different types of girls. Formal recruitment may appeal to girls who are brand new to campus and are looking to get involved or girls that chose to wait a year to get to know the chapters better but are now ready to dive in. On the other hand, Continuous Open Bidding may appeal to girls who didn't feel prepared to rush in the fall, girls who are new students in the Spring semester, and girls who wanted to take a semester to get comfortable with campus before recruitment.

Furthermore, freshmen may feel pressured into joining a sorority they don't particularly like due to the fact that they think that their first year in college is the only time they are able to join a sorority. Remember, it isn't too late to join a sorority in your sophomore and junior years. There is no need to pressure yourself into a sorority you do not have your heart set on.

Time to Prep

~ 30 ~

Every PNM stresses about how to get ready for rush week, but what you may not know is that chapter women spend months and months preparing to meet you! In every house, members work all spring/summer to prepare the house for each party and the sisters for each PNM. You may be nervous to enter all these different houses and talk to girls you've never seen before in your life, but know that the girls on the other side are just as nervous and excited to talk to you! They want to make the same good impression that you want to make, and what's more, every one of those girls has gone through what you're about to go through. Each one of them understands how nervous you are and how awkward the perfectly choreographed motions of recruitment can be. They just want to get to know you as much as they can in the short time allotted to the round you're in, so take a deep breath and just be yourself! ☺

Although the beautiful décor of each house and the flawless coordination of its sisters may seem natural, decisions regarding colors, flowers, outfits, and even hairstyles are made months in advance. During the school year when the sorority's officers are appointed and elected, one sister is usually chosen to oversee the organization of next year's recruitment. This sister's title is often "Recruitment Chair" or "Head of Membership." It is her job to decide what colors and styles of clothing will be worn by the sisters during each round, what photos and decorations will be shown throughout the house, and what songs, cheers, and skits will be performed during recruitment. The Recruitment Chair usually has a committee who helps her make these decisions and execute them.

This committee will consider what color schemes will complement the house, and the sisters. When the

Recruitment Committee agrees on these decisions, they notify the rest of the chapter, explaining what types of outfits and shoes will be worn for each round, thus allowing the chapter members enough time to shop for suitable clothes throughout rest of the year. Members are often required to have their outfits approved by the committee, and sometimes are even told to buy a certain pair of shoes or item of clothing for a particular round.

Meanwhile, another sister will be put in charge of all the paper requirements in preparing for recruitment. This sister has the responsibility of gathering letters of recommendations, resumes, photos, and eventually all of the registration information for the potential new members. Friends and family who are alumni of a particular chapter are able to write recommendations for girls that they know and PNMs are usually asked to submit a resume and photo to their school's Panhellenic

Recruitment website. This process allows the sorority to gather some information about the girls that will be going through the recruitment process before this process actually starts. It also allows the chapter to identify girls who are highly recommended or are legacies, or girls whose mothers or grandmothers were sisters of that particular sorority.

With all of this information, the sister in charge of the logistical side of recruitment is able to prep other sisters about the accomplishments, hobbies, and activities of incoming PNS. This sister is also able to match PNMs with sisters who they may be compatible with throughout the different rounds of recruitment. Throughout rush week you may be surprised to find that you share many common interests and hobbies with the girl who is rushing you. This is a sign that you were matched well based on your resume and/or letters of recommendation that were written for you!

You may also notice the oddly choreographed movements of the sisters in each round. While these seemingly mechanical greetings and motions may be disconcerting, they are intentional! At most schools, chapter women gather the week before recruitment get everything ready for rush week. This time is usually referred to as "Spirit Week." During this time, each chapter prepare for the next week in various ways. They learn the songs, skits, and cheers that go along with each round as well as the physical movements through the house that will allow for each pair of girls to make the most of their time in each round. They will go over what kinds of conversations are appropriate for which rounds and will even physically practice each round, with either imaginary PNMs or other chapter women pretending to be

PNMs. This is also a time for the sisters to bond and get ready to welcome a new pledge class of wonderful ladies!

Now that you know all of this, what does it mean for you as a PNM? Knowing that sorority women prepare for recruitment for months in advance, how should you prepare yourself for this week?

One way to prepare for recruitment is to be sure to monitor what you post and what others post about you on any social media sites that you are a member of. Be sure not to curse, be crude, or post inappropriate photos on Facebook, twitter, Instagram, or any other site you are involved with.

Appearance wise, it's a good idea to decide what clothes, shoes, and hairstyles you will wear for each round of recruitment. If you wait until the day of each round to decide what to wear, you can easily become stressed.

Throughout rush week it's very important to keep a

positive attitude as you go from party to party because the

longer rounds of recruitment may start as early as 7AM,

and can last as late 10 PM. It's difficult to keep your spirits

up if you begin the day with negativity and stress, and

knowing what you will wear for each round leaves you

with one less thing to worry about each morning.

When planning outfits, it is important to keep the

formality of each round in mind. As a general rule, as the

rounds go on the attire gets increasingly dressy. Your

school's Panhellenic website probably has guidelines

about what to wear under their recruitment section. It is

good to take these guidelines into consideration, but for

the most part PNMs will wear dressier clothes to each

round. For instance, if the website tells you to wear shorts

for round one; most girls will go with either a skirt or a

casual dress. It's also good to remember that you are

dressing to impress girls, not boys. You should try to pick flattering outfits that keep your cleavage, stomach, and thighs covered. While chapter women should be more concerned about your conversation with them, it can get distracting if your clothes are skimpy or if you are over-dressed/under-dressed.

Many PNMs fall under the illusion that if they don't show up for every round of recruitment sporting a string of pearls and a Lilly Pulitzer dress they will not be accepted by sorority women. This is a bad way to approach recruitment. It's much more important to express your own style in the outfits you wear than to adhere to what you believe a *sorority* woman should wear. If you love Lilly, go for it! But, if you're trendier or sportier, pick an outfit that reflects your own personal style. There are all sorts of women in every chapter, and it's always better to be yourself than to try and fit into a stereotype that doesn't actually hold true.

That being said, the attitude that you put forth to the chapter women is much more important than the clothes you wear. It's easy to get caught up and stressed out during the longs days of parties during rush week, so it's important to stay positive. Don't worry if you don't click with every girl you talk to, just keep smiling and be as friendly and engaging as possible. It isn't fun to talk to someone who is negative or mean, and the women in the houses you visit have a limited amount of time to get to know you. So, if you waste time with negativity, these girls may not get to know the awesome and fun personality you really have!

Before the recruitment process even begins you should really think about what you truly want the girls you speak with to take away from their conversation with you.

Do you want them to know you're smart? Or that you're a great friend? Or that you are fun and love to make people laugh? Decide what you want your personal mark to be based on what you value most about yourself and others. Think of what style and characteristics you want to be associated with and prepare stories that relate to what impression you wish to leave. Think of things you can say that express the key attributes you want these girls to pick up on. Although you should try not to mechanically repeat these stories like you've prepared a speech, it's good to have a few stories in mind before you go into recruitment. When you have decided what impression you wish to give, you should attempt to tailor your resume based on these ideals so that any alumni who write you letters of recommendation will reflect these same ideals in the letters they write.

It's Just the Beginning:

Open Houses

The first round of recruitment can be the scariest—your first day of rush, your first party, your first interactions with chapter women. As you are thrown into the strange world of formal recruitment it's easy to become overwhelmed with round one, but you shouldn't be scared! First round, also referred to as open houses and/or ice tea parties, is the most casual and the shortest round of formal recruitment. The only round in which you go to every house, round one usually lasts about twenty minutes and seems even quicker!

The open house round usually consists of a short house tour and sometimes a small speech or skit. The speech or skit will give an overview of the chapter's involvement, activities, and social functions. Don't worry if you feel that most houses sound extremely similar! This is because every chapter does fun things and is full of incredible women, and the first round is not long enough to really show individual ways in which the different houses shine. As you walk through the different houses, there will probably be rooms opened up and decorated and you may even be introduced to a house mom or two. Although this is your first time seeing the inside of the houses, and there are beautiful decorations and pictures on all the walls, you really need to concentrate on your conversation with the chapter woman who is showing you around. As you look for a sisterhood to join, your connections with the chapter women is what will really point you to the right house.

In each house, you will have a limited amount of time to talk to the sister who is showing you around. Because of the time constraint, rarely will this conversation get deep and personal. Common questions will include your major, the previous summer, and things that you enjoyed in high school. As you get through a few parties you might notice that you're asking and answering the same questions over and over again. If this gets tedious for you, it's definitely getting boring for the chapter women too! You want your conversation to stand out and be enjoyable for both you and the sister you're talking to. Don't feel like you have to let the sister do all the talking; when she asks you what your major is, answer her, but then direct the conversation towards something that's fun to talk about! If you like to bake, talk about baking! If you are obsessed with Harry Potter, ask the chapter woman if she and her sisters ever get together and watch their favorite movies! If you have any questions about the house or the sisterhood, don't be afraid to ask. As much as you don't want the conversation to be awkward, neither does the girl you are talking to. When you are helping to keep things flowing in the conversation, it's easier on the sister, which will leave her with a good impression of you!.

But, you have to be careful! There are some questions that will not leave a good impression. One of the worst things you can ask a sorority woman about is a question about another sorority. A good general rule is to not to mention any house other than the one you are in. Whether it's good or bad, if you are talking about another house, the sister you are speaking to will feel that you aren't really interested in her chapter. Another good rule of thumb is to try not to talk about partying. Although a sorority is a social organization, chapter women want to know that you are interested in making lifelong friends, not just drinking and meeting boys. If the sister brings it up, you don't need to freak out and change the subject, but make sure that she knows that you're interested in everything that being in a sorority comes with, not just the social aspect. Remember that round one is short, so try to stay away from inappropriate or touchy subjects and just keep it light!

At the end of the round, after going into every house and talking to only one or two women from each chapter, you will be asked to preference them. This means that you will have to narrow down the number of houses that you would like to visit again. For most PNMs eliminating houses during the first round can be very difficult. However, because you are considering such a large number of chapters and have only spent a short amount of time in each, it is hard to know which houses you liked and didn't like. This is why it is imperative that you write notes about each house after you visit it! Write down how you felt, what stood out to you, something to remember the girl you talked to...anything to help you differentiate between houses. This is also a good time to talk to your recruitment counselors! They have all gone through recruitment and are trained to help you out! Although your counselors shouldn't sway you towards one house over another, they can help you sort out your own feelings. They can also clue you in to what to expect while inside the houses and in further rounds, and are usually equipped with toiletry items, water, and snacks to help you throughout the day.

That being said, the first rounds of formal recruitment are usually very long, strenuous days. That means that you need to get plenty of sleep and show up in the morning prepared for the long day ahead. Because formal recruitment often occurs at the beginning of the fall semester, the weather can get very unpredictable. It may be unbearably hot, or even rainy! It's good to pack an umbrella and bring extra deodorant as well as sweat sheets for your face.

Some girls even buy handheld fans to keep things breezy between parties. Be sure to bring extra lip-gloss, mints, and extra shoes for walking if you think yours will get uncomfortable! Although your recruitment counselors will probably have some snacks for you and you will usually get at least one break for lunch, definitely pack some snacks so that you have enough energy to make it through the day. It's important to take care of yourself throughout the week so that you can devote yourself to finding the sisterhood that will make your college years unforgettable!

Time to Party:

Recruitment Parties

Whew! You made it past the first round, and now you have fewer houses to visit and longer parties to go to! The narrowing down stage between rounds began when you made your preference list the night before. Formal recruitment is a mutual process though, so all of the houses you visited also had to make a list of the girls that they wanted to see again in the next round. Part of your school's Panhellenic Council will be officers who are in charge of overseeing and organizing recruitment, and one of these officers will be in charge of its technical aspect. She will take the lists from your Recruitment Counselors and the lists from the houses and plug them into a computer to compile your schedule for the next round. If all of the houses that you have preferenced want to invite you back, your schedule will include all of these houses. Often though, because there are so many girls and so many houses, this does not happen. If one of the houses that you wanted to return to did not put you on their list,

that house will not be on your schedule. But if that is the

case and one of the houses that you did not want to go

back to asked to see you again, they may be on your

schedule the next day.

The computer arranges it so that you visit the most

houses that you can, whether they are all the houses that

you picked or not. That being said, PNMs are not

guaranteed to have a full schedule. If a full schedule is to

visit eleven houses, your schedule can have eight houses,

five houses, or even just one house. Some girls, if they go

into recruitment with a bad attitude or just don't really

seem like they're going to click anywhere, may even get

dropped from every house. This is very rare, but it can

happen! Whether you have all slots full or only a few

houses to visit again, it's good to not get too caught up in

which houses dropped or kept you for this round. Each

house has to narrow down the number of girls they ask

back after every round, and at this point in recruitment,

the chapter women have only gotten to talk to you for a

very short amount of time. Trust me, it's not personal if

they did not invite you back, although you don't know it

yet, you're probably a great fit somewhere else!

Another thing to keep in mind is that because

you've only been to each house once, it's very likely that

your favorite house after round one will not be the house

you end up at. As you spend more time in each house and

talk to more sisters, you will get a better feel for the

different sororities and what they stand for. This will

make it easier to know where you will feel most

comfortable and where you want to end up on bid day.

Knowing this, it's important not to get too upset if a house

you really liked dropped you. Just like in the first round,

you need to keep a positive attitude so that you can really

be present in all of your conversations with the chapter women you speak to during round two. If you are upset or worried that will shine through in the way you act and speak, and this may leave the chapter woman with a negative impression of you. So don't worry, as crazy and stressful as this process is, it really works! So trust it, and after everything is said and done you will end up at the place you were really meant to be.

Round two can vary among different schools, but the emphasis is often on the particular sorority's philanthropy. After you enter the house again, the Philanthropy Chair or even the President may stand up and speak about the cause that their chapter raises money for and the way that they raise the money. However, because of this focus, girls who are rushing you may stick to this topic, but that is not required! This is also the round that many chapter women choose to speak about other ways that their chapter gets involved throughout campus. Although this round is longer than the first, conversation is still light. This is especially true because in many houses the sisters will use a tactic called bumping. Often the girl who welcomes you into the house will be interrupted by another sister after a few minutes of conversation. The first girl you were speaking with will then excuse herself, and the second girl will continue talking to you. This transition is known as a bump. In some houses you may even be bumped by two or three girls! This allows more girls to get to know you and form an opinion of you. In one sense, it's good because you will get a better feel of the house in general, and they can get a better feel for you, but at the same time, it makes each conversation shorter, so try and make the most of each one!

At the end of this round you will have to decrease the number of houses on your list again. At this point you should have a better feel for each house, but try to keep an open mind! A lot can still change in the rounds that follow.

Third Round is one of the most important rounds! The same narrowing down process that occurred between the first and second rounds has happened again, but after this round you will have to narrow your houses down to the three (at some schools, four) houses that you want to Pref at! This round is even longer than the second round, and now that you've been to each of these houses twice already, you should really be getting to know the different personalities and strengths of each different house. Also, you will usually be talking to the one girl for this entire round, which allows you to have a more personal conversation and discuss more weighty subjects.

At most schools the third round is the sisterhood round, and each chapter usually shows a short video or slide show to try and show you what sisterhood means to them. These presentations are often equipped with mushy songs and heartwarming video clips. Watching them, a lot of PNMs and sisters get emotional, even tearing up. You shouldn't feel like you have to cry just because other people are, but if something moves you then go with it! During this round the sister who is speaking to you may tell you a story about experiences that she has had with her sisters. She will try and explain the special way that her chapter's sisterhood is different from any others. Again, this chapter woman may become emotional, but don't feel awkward or embarrassed! She is just trying to show you what being in that sorority means to her. She may also ask you what you are looking for in a sisterhood. This is your opportunity to explain what you want in a sorority and ask her questions to find out if her sisterhood will meet your needs!

Sometimes awkward things happen during these rounds. A bump may catch you off guard or transition strangely. A sister may trip or fall. You may even trip or fall! Anything can happen! With so many people trying to move around in a relatively small space, people are bound to bump into things or even other people. If something like this happens, you just have to go with it and remember that everyone is human. If the chapter woman you are speaking to does something embarrassing, ask her if she is ok, or empathize with her saying that things like that happen to you all the time. Don't make a big deal out of it, but don't ignore it either, because that makes things even more awkward sometimes.

Sometimes conversations can get awkward too. If you accidentally say something that might sound scandalous, drop a bad word, or mention partying a little too much, you may think that the chapter woman with you will just write you off. Don't worry, you can fix it! Make sure that you let the sister know that you aren't an ordinarily crude person, and try and let her know that you're really looking for more than just a way to go to parties and meet boys. Ask questions about the sisterhood and the bonds that she has with her sisters, and maybe even throw in a few compliments! Say something like, "I can tell that you guys are all so close and I just really hope I find something just as special." Everyone likes to hear nice things about themselves! If you change the subject and talk about deeper subjects, the sister rushing you will be sure to forget your slip up in no time

<u>It's a Strong Bond:</u>

<u>Preference Day</u>

It's preference day! So close to the end! Prefs can be scary. This is the longest and most formal round, and it's the last chance to talk to the sisters and learn more about the house before you are faced with a final decision. The attire for this round is usually cocktail dress/formal. This means that you should definitely wear a dress and heals. The dress should be formal enough to wear to a Homecoming dance or fancy Sweet Sixteen party. Make sure whatever you pick is not too short, tight, or low cut. Remember, you want the other girls to like it! You should try not to pick anything too flashy either. Many girls go with classy black dresses and heels, but any color is fine! Pick something that shows off your own personal style, but that's still classy, appropriate, and comfortable to sit and walk around in!

Prefs can get a little intimidating, because this is the round that houses usually share a small part of their ritual to the girls still left visiting in this final round. A sorority's ritual includes its secret songs, word, and ceremonies based on the particular sorority's fundamental values and beliefs. These rituals are the common thread that pulls together women from across the nation, throughout many generations, and are held near and dear to many sorority women. It is very special for the chapter women to share a small part of this ritual with you during prefs, so it's a very serious moment of recruitment. Rituals can consist of dark rooms, candlelight, slow songs, and even may incorporate some of the sorority's symbols. The ceremony that they share with you may seem strange, but don't be scared! None of these rituals will hurt you or anyone involved in them!

Even more than third round, many people will become very emotional during the ritual and even after or before while they are talking to you. PNMs also find themselves crying at times. A lot of times girls expect to cry when they find the house that they feel is their best fit, almost looking towards this emotion as a personal signal to what house they should choose. It's important to remember that people experience emotions in very different ways. Just because another girl is crying and you are not does not mean that this house is a fit for her and not for you! You may never have that breaking-down moment when tears fall from your eyes and you know you're home. But that's ok! A lot of the girls who are crying don't know why they're crying and probably will have just as difficult of a decision as you will. On the other hand, if you feel really moved and emotional, just go with it! The chapter women will not judge you, and it's better to express your emotions so that they know how you feel about their house.

The conversations during pref rounds are also the most serious. If you are a legacy, you may receive a letter from your mom, sister, or whomever during this time. Often, the girl who speaks to you will be someone you already know, someone from your hometown, or someone that you have had a strong connection with sometime previously during the week. At this point of recruitment, most houses really like and want to see you the next day on their lawn. The girl who is rushing you is probably working her hardest to sell you on the house you're in because it's so close to bid day! This is the time to ask any questions you may have or voice any concerns you have about a particular house or sorority life in general. Remember, this is the last chance to get a feel for the girls in each house. Pay special attention not only to the way that the girl rushing you makes you feel, but also the way that you have felt throughout the week.

After your parties are over, you may have the hardest decision of your life. If you are lucky, pref round will solidify the choice in your mind and make your rankings clear. Most girls are not this lucky, and may be left sitting with their Recruitment Counselor for hours talking things out. You have to consider where you feel the most comfortable, where you had the most fun talking to the girls, and where you can see yourself hanging around in the house and smiling in the picture on the walls. Another good thing to pay attention to is the other PNMs around you at each house. By prefs, chances are that about a third of the girls at each party you go to will be with you at bid day the next day! Try to decipher whether you thought the girls who rushed you really cared about you or just wanted you to think their house was the best. Were they trying to help you through this rough week? Or were they just trying to impress you? Overall, the best advice I can give you is to go with your first

instinct; it's usually what you really want! If you follow

your heart and keep an open mind throughout the week of

recruitment, everything will work out for the best on bid

day!

<u>Home Sweet Home:</u>

<u>Bid Day</u>

Yay! The day has finally arrived....Bid Day! Bid Day will probably be one of the most exciting days of your life. After a week of stress, you will finally know which sisterhood you will be a part of for the rest of your life! Bid Day usually consists of a general assembly in which you will find out what houses your Recruitment Counselors are in and receive your bid cards. Everyone will open their bid cards at the same time, finding out what house they have gotten a bid from! After bid cards are opened, different schools do different things. In some schools girls divide into groups and take buses to the houses, at other schools the girls all just run home to their houses, and at some schools everyone stays in one general location for bid day activities. You and the rest of the girls who have gotten bids from the same sorority will make up the sorority's new pledge class! Be sure to be friendly and start getting to know your pledge sisters as soon as you can. You will probably be close with these girls for the rest of your life! No matter what your school's bid day procedure is, it will be full of excitement, squealing, and hugs!

For the most part, immediately after you receive your bid there will be some sort of bid day party. Most houses have a system of bid day buddies, in which an older girl will be designated to find you, introduce herself, and show you around that day and the rest of your first week or so in the sorority. At the party, your bid day buddy will usually come find you and take you into the party. The house will be decorated, there is usually yummy food, and there will be tons of girls taking pictures! A lot of times you will also be greeted with bid day gifts! Although this time is incredibly exciting, it can also be overwhelming! Some new members will know other girls who have also gotten bids, but if you don't know anyone else, it may be intimidating to run into a house full of girls you haven't met yet. Also, you may be physically and emotionally exhausted after the long week of parties. Don't worry if every girl you see isn't your best friend. I promise that even if it takes a while to get to know the girls around you, you will find some of your best friends here! The girls in your pledge class will grow and experience college right alongside you, and you will share a special bond that no one else has, or ever will have!

Getting a bid means that you are invited to pledge the particular sorority. You are not a sister yet, but rather a new member or pledge. Pledging for girls joining sororities is a very different process than pledging for boys joining fraternities. While hazing is very common in fraternities, this is not the case in sororities. Instead, lots of presents and fun events are planned for the new pledges of each sorority! Soon after bid day most houses will host a New Member retreat, in which you will get to know your pledge class and learn more about what it means to be a part of the sorority you pledge. There will also be fun sisterhood events and pledge socials organized for your pledge class in which you will get to know each other. Later, your pledge class will probably attend weekly or biweekly meetings in which you will learn about the expectations, traditions, and organization of your sorority. These meetings will end after about 6-8 weeks when you are initiated. After initiation, you will be shown the entirety of the ritual and you will be a sister of the sorority that you were pledging!

The first couple of weeks will be a whirlwind! So much exciting things are happening and you are meeting tons of great new people. Everything is fun and new, but you have to remember that joining a sorority comes with certain responsibilities. You will be expected to pay dues, to attend meetings (particularly a weekly meeting called chapter), and most importantly you will be expected to represent your sorority in a respectable way. After you join a sorority, anything you do and say will reflect back on that sorority, both good and bad. You will benefit from being a part of a nationally known organization with a good reputation and connections throughout the country. This organization also wants to benefit from having you as a member. Joining a sorority is one of the most life changing and wonderful experiences in college that you can have, but it also come with responsibilities and expectations that you must be willing to comply with. That being said, for a lifelong sisterhood, these responsibilities and expectations are definitely not too much to handle ☺

Now that you've found a sisterhood that you want to be a part of, you probably want to know what's next. If you want to make the most of your Greek life, it's important to start early! You will be spending a lot of time with your pledge sisters, so you will get to know them pretty quickly, but it's also important to get to know girls in older pledge classes as well. In most sororities it isn't mandatory to attend every event, and many girls pick and choose events that sound fun. If you are looking to become a leader in your chapter it is good to go to as many events as possible! Especially the ones in which you could see yourself having a larger role. If you could see yourself as the future social chair, go to every social event! If you love service, make sure you volunteer to participate in all of the different philanthropic opportunities that are available to you. If you want to eventually run for an executive position in the chapter, step up and join committees or smaller assistant roles and work your way up! Use the attitudes and

conversation skills that you've acquired for rush as you start

your journey for the next four years. These will be the most

exciting years of your life, and only you can decide how they

will turn out!

Top 10 Do's and Don'ts for Recruitment

1. DON'T post anything inappropriate on social media sites before recruitment.

2. DO prepare for recruitment! Plan what outfits you will wear and what topics you will bring up with the chapter women!

3. DON'T be nervous about meeting sisters, they can't wait to meet you and get to know you!

4. DO be yourself!

5. DON'T interrupt, talk about boys or booze, or ask yes/no questions!

6. DO take good notes after each house you visit.

7. DON'T talk about other houses than the one you are in!

8. DO ask questions and articulate any worries you have.

9. DON'T stress if you don't immediately know what house you want to join.

10. DO keep an open mind and follow your heart!

Sorority Profiles

Alpha Chi Omega

Established: 1885

Philanthropy: Alpha Chi Omega foundation, Domestic Violence Awareness

Headquarters: Indianapolis, IN

Website: www.alphachiomega.org

Motto: Together Let Us Seek the Heights

Mission: Enrich the lives of members through lifetime opportunities for friendship, leadership leaning, and service.

Symbol: Golden Lyre

Colors: Scarlet Red, Olive Green

Flower: Red Carnation

Jewel: Pearl

Greek Patron: Hera

Notable Alumni:

Melissa Rycroft – Reality show star

Deidre Downs – Miss America 2005

Carol Duvall – The Carroll Duval Show host

Condoleezza Rice – Former U.S. Secretary of State

Trista Rehn Sutter – Former Bachelorette star

Meredith Monroe – Dawson's Creek Actress

Alpha Delta Pi

Established: 1851

Philanthropy: Ronald McDonald House

Headquarters: Atlanta, GA

Website: www.alphadeltapi.org

Motto: We Live for Each Other

Mascot: "Alphie" the Lion

Colors: Azure Blue & White

Flower: Woodland Violet

Jewel: Diamond

Notable Alumni:

Kate Capshaw – Actress and Wife of Steven Spielberg

Deana Carter – Country Singer

Karen Fairchild – Singer, Member of Little Big Town

Nancy Grace – News Host

Danica McKellar – The Wonder Years Actress

Emily Procter – Actress

Michelle Pfeiffer – Actress

Kathy Bates – Actress

Alpha Gamma Delta

Established: 1904

Philanthropy: Alpha Gamma Delta Foundation

Headquarters: Indianapolis, IN

Website: www.alphagammadelta.org

Motto: Live with Purpose

Mascot: Squirrel

Colors: Red, Buff, Green

Flower: Red & Buff Roses with Green Asparagus Ferns

Jewel: Pearl

Notable Alumni:

Amber Brkich – Reality show star

Gloria Loring – Actress

Karen McCullah Lutz – Screenwriter

Barbara Jo Walker – Miss America 1947

Rita Coolidge – Singer

Fran Allison – Radio and TV Personality

Donna Fargo – Singer

Dorothy Provine – Actress

Alpha Epsilon Phi

Established: 1909

Philanthropy: Elizabeth Glaser Pediatric AIDS Foundation, Sharsharet

Headquarters: Danburry, CT

Website: www.aephi.org

Motto: Many Hearts, One Purpose

Mascot: Giraffe

Colors: Green & White

Flower: Lily of the Valley

Jewel: Pearl

Symbol: Columns

Notable Alumni:

Lillian Copeland – Olympic Gold and Silver Medalist

Elizabeth Glaser – AIDS Activist

Nancy Goodman Brinker – Founder of Susan G. Komen Foundation

Erica Hill – News Anchor

Charlotte Rae – Actress

Judith Resnik – 2nd woman Astronaut

Dinah Shore – Talk Show Host

Alpha Omicron Pi

Established: 1897

Philanthropy: Arthritis Research & Education

Headquarters: Brentwood, TN

Website: www.alphaomicronpi.org

Motto: Women Enriched Through Lifelong Friendship

Mascot: Panda

Colors: Cardinal

Flower: Jacqueminot Rose

Jewel: Ruby

Notable Alumni:

Jennifer Wallen – Reality star on The Apprentice

Katie Allen – Wife of American Idol Kris Allen

Cathy Grimes – Reality star on The Bachelor

Aneta Corsaut – Actress

Mercedes Farhat – 2008 Olympic Swimmer

Courtney Kupets – Olympic Gymnast

Parvati Shallow – Reality Star on Survivor

Heather Whitestone – Miss America 1995

Alpha Phi

Established: 1872

Philanthropy: Alpha Phi Foundation

Headquarters: Evanston, IL

Website: www.alphaphi.org

Motto: Union Hand in Hand

Mascot: Phi Bear

Colors: Bordeaux & Silver

Flower: Lily of the Valley & Forget Me Not

Symbol: Ivy

Notable Alumni:

Andrea Wong – Former CEO for Lifetime Television

Rosemarie DeWitt – Actress

Mildred Dunnock – Academy award nominated actress

Eliza Orlins – Reality Star on Survivor

Jeri Ryan – Actress

Inga Swenson – Tony award nominated actress

Jennifer Tisdale – Actress

Kimberly Williams Paisley – Actress and Wife of Brad Paisley

Alpha Sigma Alpha

Established: 1901

Philanthropy: Special Olympics

Headquarters: Indianapolis, IN

Website: www.alphasigmaalpha.org

Motto: Aspire, Seek, Attain

Mascot: Dot the ladybug

Colors: Crimson, Pearl White, Palm Green, Gold

Flower: Narcissus & Aster

Jewel: Pearl, Ruby

Notable Alumni:

Freida J Riley – Teacher influenced Rocket Boys in the movie October Sky

Hannah Blaylock – Singer

Christi Lukasiak – Cast member on Dance Moms

Alpha Sigma Tau

Established: 1899

Philanthropy: Pine Mountain Settlement School, Habitat for Humanity

Headquarters: Indianapolis, IN

Website: www.alphasigmatau.org

Motto: Active, Self-Reliant, Trustworthy

Colors: Emerald Green & Gold

Flower: Yellow Rose

Jewel: Pearl

Symbol: Anchor

Notable Alumni:

Terri Utley – Miss USA 1982

Sally Jesse Raphael – Talk Show Host

Gwen Frostic- Environmentalist

Alpha Xi Delta

Established: 1893

Philanthropy: Autism Speaks

Headquarters: Indianapolis, IN

Website: www.alphaxidelta.org

Motto: The pen is mightier than the sword.

Vision: Inspiring women to realize their potential

Mascot: BetXi Bear

Colors: Light Blue, Dark Blue, Gold

Flower: Pink Rose

Jewel: Pearl, Diamond

Symbol: Quill

Notable Alumni:

Laurie Lea Schaefer – Miss America 1972

Jen Schefft – Reality show star

Kelley Earnhardt Elledge – VP JR Motorsports

Verna Kay Gibson – First female CEO of a fortune 500 company

Betsey Johnson – Fashion Designer

Jan Davis – Astronaut

Chi Omega

Established: 1895

Philanthropy: Make-A-Wish-Foundation

Headquarters: Memphis, TN

Website: www.chiomega.org

Motto: Hellenic culture and Christian Ideals

Mascot: Owl

Colors: Cardinal & Straw

Flower: White Carnation

Jewel: Pearl, Diamond

Symbol: Skull & Crossbones

Notable Alumni:

Lucy Liu – Actress

Sela Ward – Actress

Joanne Woodward – Actress

Harper Lee – Author of To Kill a Mockingbird

Blanche Lambert Lincoln – US Senator

Angela Kinsey – Actress on The Office

Pat Head Summit – Women's Basketball Hall of Fame Inductee

Delta Delta Delta

Established: 1888

Philanthropy: St. Jude Children's Hospital

Headquarters: Arlington, TX

Website: www.tridelta.org

Motto: Let Us Steadfastly Love One Another

Mascot: Dolphin

Colors: Silver, Gold, Cerulean Blue

Flower: Pansy

Jewel: Pearl

Notable Alumni:

Elizabeth Dole – US Senator

Leeza Gibbons – Talk Show Host

Farrah Fawcett – Actress

Molly Sims – Actress and Model

Hoda Kotb – News Anchor

Deborah Norville – News Anchor

Katie Couric – News Anchor

Liz Claiborne – Fashion Designer

Delta Gamma

Established: 1873

Philanthropy: Service for Sight

Headquarters: Columbus, OH

Website: www.deltagamma.org

Motto: Do Good

Mascot: Hannah Doll

Colors: Bronze, Pink, Blue

Flower: Delta Gamma Cream Colored Rose

Symbol: Anchor

Notable Alumni:

Sabrina Bryan – Disney Star

Judith Ford – Miss America 1969

Mary Frann – Actress

Samantha Harris – Actress and TV Host

Patricia Heaton – Actress

Judy Bell - First female president of United States Golf Association

Rachel Ray – TV Personality and Chef

Julia Louis-Dreyfus – Emmy award winning Actress

Delta Phi Epsilon

Established: 1917

Philanthropy: Delta Phi Epsilon Education Foundation, Cystic Fibrosis Foundation, National Association of anorexia Nervosa & Associated Disorders

Headquarters: Philadelphia, PA

Website: www.dphie.org

Motto: To be rather than to seem to be.

Colors: Royal purple, Pure gold

Flower: Purple Iris

Jewel: Pearl

Symbol: Unicorn

Notable Alumni:

Stephanie Abrams – Meteorologist

Bette Midler – Grammy, Tony and Golden Globe winning Actress

Barbara Aronstein Black – 1st Woman to head Ivy League Law

Phyllis Kossoff – Cystic Fibrosis Foundation co-founder

Offira Navon – Former First Lady of Israel

Barbara Boxer – US Senator

Delta Zeta

Established: 1902

Philanthropy: Speech and Hearing; The Painted Turtle, The Starkey Hearing Foundation

Headquarters: Oxford, OH

Website: www.deltazeta.org

Mascot: Turtle

Colors: Rose & Green

Flower: Pink Killarney Rose

Jewel: Diamond

Symbol: Roman Lamp

Notable Alumni:

Marti Dodson – Lead singer for Saving Jane

Florence Henderson – Brady Bunch Actress

Joy Behar – Talk Show Host

Pat Priest – Actress

Martha Sofia Lovisa Dagmar Thyra – Princess Martha of Sweden

Kay Yow – Women's Basketball Coach

Edith Head – Emmy award winning costume designer

Melissa Ordway - Actress

Gamma Phi Beta

Established: 1874

Philanthropy: Camp Fire, Girl Guides of Canada and Girls on the Run

Headquarters: Centennial, CO

Website: www.gammaphibeta.org

Motto: Founded upon a rock.

Colors: Brown & Mode

Flower: Pink Carnation

Symbol: Crescent Moon

Notable Alumni:

Kristin Chenoweth – Tony and Emmy award winning Actress

Meagan Holder – Actress

Heather McDonald – Actress, Comedy writer for Chelsea Lately

Kelli O'Hara – Tony award nominated Actress

Kelli McCarty – Miss USA 1991

Mary Beth Peil – Dawson's Creek Actress

Hope Summers – The Andy Griffith Show Actress

Dr. Laurel Clark – NASA Astronaut

Cloris Leachman – Academy award winning actress

Kappa Alpha Theta

Established: 1870

Philanthropy: CASA Court Appointed Special Advocates

Headquarters: Indianapolis, IN

Website: www.kappaalphatheta.org

Motto: True Promise

Colors: Black & Gold

Flower: Black & Gold Pansy

Symbol: Kite & Twin Stars

Notable Alumni:

Tory Burch – Fashion Designer

Amy Grant – Grammy award winning singer

Laura Bush – Former First Lady of the United States of America

Lynne Cheney – Former Second Lady of the United States of America

Kerri Strug – Olympic Gymnast

Sheryl Crow – Grammy award winning Singer

Joan Ganz Cooney – Sesame Street Creator

Melissa Stark – News Reporter

Kappa Delta

Established: 1897

Philanthropy: Girl Scouts of the USA, Prevent Child Abuse America, Orthopedic Research Awards, Children's Hospital of Richmond Virginia

Headquarters: Memphis, TN

Website: www.kappadelta.org

Motto: Let us strive for that which is honorable, beautiful, and highest.

Colors: Olive green, Pearl White

Flower: White Rose

Jewel: Diamond, Emerald, Pearl

Symbol: Nautilus Shell, Dagger, Teddy Bear, Katydid

Notable Alumni:

Annie Anderson – TV Personality

Ellen Albertini Dow – Actress

Ali Landry – Miss USA 1996

Debbie Maffett Wilson – Miss America 1983

Leigh Anne Roberts Tuohy – Subject of The Blind Side

Suzy Spafford – Suzy's Zoo Greeting Cards Creator

Vera Bradley – Fashion Designer

Kappa Kappa Gamma

Established: 1870

Philanthropy: Reading is Fundamental

Headquarters: Columbus, OH

Website: www.kappa.org

Motto: Tradition of Leadership, Aspire to Be

Colors: Dark Blue, Light Blue

Flower: Fleur-de-Lis

Jewel: Sapphire

Symbol: Key

Notable Alumni:

Kate Spade – Fashion Designer

Sophia Bush – One Tree Hill Actress

Ashley Judd – Actress

Nancy O'Dell – Television Host

Jane Pauley – Television Journalist

Lo Bosworth – The Hills Reality show star

Donna DeVarona – Gold Medal Olympic Swimmer

Charolette York (The Character) – Sex & The City

Phi Mu

Established: 1852

Philanthropy: Children's Miracle Network

Headquarters: Peachtree City, GA

Website: www.Phimu.org

Motto: The Faithful Sisters

Mascot: The Lion "Sir Fidel"

Colors: Rose & White

Flower: Rose Color Carnation

Symbol: Quatrefoil

Notable Alumni:

Susan Harling – Inspiration for Steel Magnolias

Mary Wickes – Actress

Kimberly Schlapman – Singer, Member of Little Big Town

Jerrie Mock – First woman to fly solo around the world

Mary Weber – Astronaut

Pat Mitchell – PBS President

Kathryn Stockett – The Help Author

Debbie Phelps – Mother of Olympic Swimmer Michael Phelps

Phi Sigma Sigma

Established: 1913

Philanthropy: Phi Sigma Sigma Foundation

Headquarters: Elkridge, Maryland

Website: www.phisigmasigma.org

Motto: Aim High

Colors: King Blue, Gold

Flower: American Beauty Rose

Jewel: Sapphire

Notable Alumni:

Irna Phillips – Mother of modern Soap Opera

Shannon Ford – Mrs. USA 2011

Tatyana McFadden – Six time Paralympic Medalist

Alex Flinn – New York Times Best Selling Author

Pi Beta Phi

Established: 1867

Philanthropy: Literacy,
Champions Are Readers (CAR),
Arrowmont,
Arrow in the Arctic

Headquarters: Town & Country Missouri

Website: www.pibetaphi.org

Symbol: Arrow

Color: Wine, Silver Blue

Flower: Wine Carnation

Notable Alumni:

Susan Akin – Miss America 1986

Faye Dunaway – Academy award winning Actress

Jennifer Garner – Golden Globe winning actress

Kathy Garver – Actress

Courtney Gibbs – Miss USA 1988

Barbara Bush – Former First Lady, USA

Grace Coolidge – Former First Lady, USA

Margaret Truman – Daughter of President Harry Truman

Sigma Delta Tau

Established: 1917

Philanthropy: Prevent Child Abuse America

Headquarters: Carmel, Indiana

Website: www.sigmadeltatau.com

Motto: One hope of many people

Symbol: Torch

Colors: Café, Old Blue

Flower: Golden Tea Rose

Jewel: Lapis Lazuli

Mascot: Teddy Bear

Notable Alumni:

Joyce Brothers – Psychologist

Christy Carlson Romano – Even Stevens Actress

Sherry Lansing – CEO Paramount Pictures

Terry Savage – Author

Marilyn Salenger – Emmy award winning Anchor

Lynn Price – Social Entrepreneur

Sigma Kappa

Established: 1874

Philanthropy: Sigma Kappa Foundation, Inherit the Earth, Gerontology research, Maine Sea Coast Mission, Alzheimer's Disease research

Headquarters: Indianapolis, Indiana

Website: www.sigmakappa.org

Motto: One heart, one way

Colors: Maroon, Lavender

Flower: Wild Purple Violet

Jewel: Pearl

Notable Alumni:

Susan Eisenhower – Granddaughter of President Dwight D. Eisenhower

Maitland Ward –Boy Meets World Actress

Lauren Roman – Actress

Renee Duprel – Olympic Cyclist

Sigma Sigma Sigma

Established: 1898

Philanthropy: The Sigma Sigma Sigma Foundation

Headquarters: Woodstock, Virginia

Website: www.sigmasigmasigma.org

Motto: Faithful Unto Death

Symbol: Sailboat

Colors: Royal Purple, White

Flower: Purple Violet

Jewel: Pearl

Notable Alumni:

Carrie Underwood – American Idol Country Singer

Linda Denham – Care Bears Creator

Lauren Lee – Biggest Loser Contestant

Billie Letts – Author

Mary Rhodes Russell –Judge

Theta Phi Alpha

Established: 1912

Philanthropy: Glenmary Home Missioners, The House That Theta Phi Alpha Built

Headquarters: Bay Village, Ohio

Website: www.thetaphialpha.org

Motto: Nothing great is ever achieved without much enduring

Mascot: Penguin

Colors: blue, gold, silver

Flower: White Rose

Jewel: Sapphire, Pearl

Symbol: Compass

Notable Alumni:

Marge Schott – CEO Cincinnati Reds

Terry Meeuwsen – Miss America 1973

Jennifer Hunter Smith – President Spiritville USA

Dr. Mari Ann Callais – CAMPUSPEAK presenter

Mollye Rees – Singer

Tisha Terrasini Banker – Actress

Zeta Tau Alpha

Established: 1898

Philanthropy: Breast Cancer Education & Awareness

Headquarters: Indianapolis, Indiana

Website: www.zetataualpha.org

Motto: Seek The Noblest

Colors: Turquoise Blue, Steel Gray

Flower: White Violet

Notable Alumni:

Erin Andrews – ESPN Anchor

Susan Ford Bales – Daughter of President Gerald Ford

Betty Buckley – Tony award winning Actress

Faith Daniels – News Personality

Phyllis George – Miss America 1971

Shannon James – Model

Geralyn Lucas – Author

Jenna Morasca – Reality show star on Survivor

Betty Nguyen – News Journalist

Lynda Bird Johnson Robb – Daughter of Lyndon B. Johnson

Get to Know Us a Little Better...

Greek Life Now is an online company created by a Greek Alumnus. This organization came from the idea to create one central website that offers everything a Greek member could need; from preparing for the first day of recruitment, all the way through graduation. This company offers a place for assistance, fun times and a great sense of community. Greek Life Now is here to assist Greek members throughout their entire Greek life experience.

Visit www.greeklifenow.com for more recruitment advice! And download a FREE recruitment cheat sheet!

3

Made in the USA
Charleston, SC
20 May 2015